INVESTING FOR TWEENS

INVESTING FOR TWEENS

Learn Essential Financial Skills to Achieve Your Money Goals

Jamie Bosse, CFP®, RFC, CCFC

Zeitgeist • New York

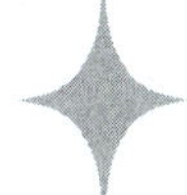

This publication contains the opinions and ideas of its author. It is intended to provide helpful and informative material on the subject matter covered. It is sold with the understanding that the author and publisher are not engaged in rendering professional services in the book. If the reader requires personal assistance or advice, a competent professional should be consulted. The author and publisher specifically disclaim any responsibility for any liability, loss, or risk, personal or otherwise, which is incurred as a consequence, directly or indirectly, of the use and application of any of the contents of this book.

Zeitgeist Young Adult
An imprint of Zeitgeist™
A division of Penguin Random House LLC
1745 Broadway, New York, NY 10019
zeitgeistpublishing.com
penguinrandomhouse.com

ISBN: 9798217151141

Printed in the United States of America
1st Printing

Illustrations © by VOOK/Shutterstock.com, Martyshova Maria/Shutterstock.com, imhaf maulana/Shutterstock.com
Book design by Aimee Fleck
Author photograph © by Nikita Razo
Edited by Sarah Curley

The authorized representative in the EU for product safety and compliance is Penguin Random House Ireland, Morrison Chambers, 32 Nassau Street, Dublin D02 YH68, Ireland. https://eu-contact.penguin.ie

To my kids and every kid reading this:

Knowledge is your superpower.

Use it to build a future you love.

CONTENTS

INTRODUCTION

MILLIONAIRE IN THE MAKING

Why Mastering Money Matters

Hi! My name is Jamie Bosse, and I have three BIG jobs: I am a mom, an author, and a financial planner. I'm raising my four kids to be money savvy. I write books for kids and adults to help them understand how money works and how to use it wisely. Now, you might be wondering, *What, exactly, is a financial planner?* Think of me as a mix of part teacher and part guide. I help families get organized and make smart money decisions so they can live the lives they want.

Now, let's talk about you. Money is an important tool you can use to buy the things you want and need. But, it can be tricky to manage, because there are so many decisions to make. What if you really want to buy something now, but you're trying to save money for something big? Should you spend your money now or save it for later? How can you make sure you don't run out of money? How do you choose whether to spend on one item or another?

Being smart with money takes practice, just like learning how to play an instrument or a new sport, and the sooner you start, the easier it'll be when you grow up. If you learn how to save, spend, invest, and make good money decisions now, you'll have less stress and more freedom with money later. This is something you can do now as a kid to make your life as an adult easier and better!

PART ONE

BUILDING YOUR FINANCIAL FOUNDATION

CHAPTER 1

MONEYMAKERS

Starting Small and Dreaming Big

Get ready to explore the world of work! In this chapter, you'll learn fun ways to earn money, the differences between having a job and starting your own business, and how to build your first résumé. You'll also get the chance to dream about the jobs you might want one day.

Cool Ways to Make Cash

Money is earned by working and providing value for someone else. This could mean working at a job, like at the grocery store bagging groceries, or providing a service for someone, like walking their dog. Here are some ways you can make money:

- Babysitting
- Dog walking
- Doing extra chores for your parents or another trusted adult
- Helping neighbors clean their garage or carry groceries
- House-sitting (watering plants; checking mail for out-of-town neighbors)
- Making and selling homemade crafts

- Making money online through a blog or YouTube channel (this takes time!)
- Selling your old bicycles, sports equipment, electronics, toys, or trading cards
- Serving as a referee/umpire for younger sports teams
- Tutoring younger kids in school subjects, instruments, or sports you're good at
- Yard work (mowing lawns, raking leaves, shoveling snow)
- Washing cars or bicycles for friends and neighbors

Figuring Out Your Fees

How much should you charge for your work?

Setting the right price for your work can be tricky, but it's an important part of running a successful business. In this section, you'll learn what to consider when deciding how much to charge your customers. This way, you can feel confident that your price is fair and financially smart.

Meet Darla. Darla loves dogs and knows all the dogs in the neighborhood. She's thinking about starting a dog-walking business, but she doesn't know how much to charge. Here are some things Darla should think about:

➜ *How much do people pay for this type of service?*

Darla shouldn't charge too much or too little. The best way to find the right price is to research what people usually pay dog walkers in her area—she can do a quick Google search or ask neighbors. If her price is too high, people won't hire her; if it's too low, she won't earn what she deserves.

➜ *How much time will it take to do the work, and what is she giving up during that time?*

With any job, you want to consider the time it takes to do it. Time is an important resource, and we have only so much time each day. Darla needs to be sure she can fit in the dog walking with her schoolwork and other activities. She may also have to give up time spent playing with friends, so she should make sure she's okay with this. If it takes 30 minutes to walk a dog, she should also make sure the fee she charges is fair for that amount of time.

→ *What supplies will she need, and how much do they cost?*

Will Darla need to buy anything to run her business? Extra leashes? Dog treats? New walking shoes? It's always important to think about the extra costs involved in your business to be sure you charge enough to cover those costs and still make some money on top of that.

→ *What is her experience with dog walking?*

Darla is new to the dog-walking business. If another dog walker in town has five years of experience, Darla may start out charging less than they do. Once she gains more experience, she can begin to increase her prices.

Darla should also reconsider her fees as she learns and grows in the business. Once she gets started, she'll know more about the costs and time it takes to do her job. She can use that knowledge to adjust her prices as needed.

ACTIVITY

Be Your Own Boss

How can you decide on the type of business you want to create? Let's explore!

Starting a business begins with knowing yourself. In this activity, you'll ask yourself questions to identify what you enjoy, what you're good at, and how you can help others. By focusing on your strengths and interests, you'll get closer to finding the perfect business idea: one that's fun and meaningful to you.

1. **Answer the following questions:**

   What are you good at (or could learn to be good at)?

   ____

   ____

   What do you like to do?

   ____

   ____

   What are some things that other people don't like to do (or can't do) that you could do for them?

   ____

   ____

What problems do others have that you can solve?

What do you hope to achieve with your business?

2. **Identify the themes you're seeing.** In Darla's case, she likes dogs, she knows how to handle them, and she knows that lots of people in her neighborhood don't have time to take their dogs for a walk. She's turning what she enjoys (and is good at) into a business to make money. How about you? Write about the ideas coming up for you.

3. **Now that you have an idea or two for your business, it's time to make a business plan!** Think about your goals, then answer the following prompts and questions:

Name your business: Choose a name that tells people what you do and adds a fun detail about you, like your name. For example, Beth's Babysitting Club.

___

Your "why": Why do you want to start this business?

___

Product: Describe the product you are selling or the service you are providing.

___

Target market: Who is your customer? Who will want to buy your products or use your services?

___

Pricing model: How much will your product cost for the customer? How much will you charge for your services? Will you charge a one-time fee for each service, or a monthly fee for ongoing service?

___

Marketing: How will people find out about your business? Social media? Email? Flyers? Word of mouth? Where will you advertise? Online or in a physical location? Write some specific places here.

___

PROS AND CONS

EMPLOYEE VERSUS ENTREPRENEUR

There are two main ways you can work to earn money: You can work in someone else's business, or you can start your own business. When you work for someone else, you are their **employee**. When you work for yourself, you are an **entrepreneur**.

An entrepreneur is someone who starts their own business. They come up with the idea, figure out how to make it work (all the things we talked about in the previous activity), and take care of everything involved in running the business. If your business needs supplies, you're responsible for buying them. If your business is struggling, you must figure out how to make it profitable. It might sound like fun to "be your own boss," and it can be, but it also takes a lot of work. There can also be a lot of rewards if your business is successful.

When you're an employee, you help someone else run their business. The person who owns the company tells you what to do. You're doing work and getting paid for it, but you don't have to worry about the details of running the business. Being an employee is a good way to earn money and learn how to work without having to make all the big (and sometimes stressful) decisions for the business.

Both ways of working are important and help our world go round! In fact, many people do both types of work at some point in their lives. They may work as an employee for a while, then decide to start their own company with what they've learned. They may even change careers entirely to create a business in an area that's totally new to them. That's the cool thing about work—you can be whatever you choose to be. And that can change over time!

Rock Your Résumé

Let's talk about a résumé: what it is, what to include on it, and how to use it to land a job that's a perfect fit for you!

What's a résumé?

A **résumé** is a document you create about yourself and present to future employers when looking for a job. Your résumé explains to a potential employer why you and your skills would be an excellent fit for the job they are offering.

A résumé shows the skills and experience you have that make you a good candidate for a job. It also lists your achievements and the things you are good at.

Here are some things that you could include in your résumé:

- **Jobs you've done before:** These can include volunteer or paid work babysitting, lawn mowing, dog walking, delivering newspapers, cleaning, tutoring, and more.
- **Skills and experience:** Maybe you're really good at math and have tutored other students. Or perhaps you're a babysitter. You can list your years of tutoring or babysitting experience, and any special experience you have, such as taking care of babies as well as older kids. Maybe you're really good at organizing or overseeing a project from start to finish. Or maybe you know a certain computer program or how to do basic coding. All of this is valuable information and makes *you* a valuable candidate for the right job.
- **Activities:** You can include any awards you have received, clubs you participate in, volunteer work, or instruments or sports you play. Employers like to know what extra things you do. It shows them that you are good at managing your time and handling lots of things at once. It also shows them that you do more than what is necessary.

OSCAR BOSSE

Lawn Care Extraordinaire

123-456-7890 Oscar@gmail.com 123 Anywhere St., Any City, ST 12345

Summary

Ambitious and hard-working 12-year-old seeking summer work in lawn care and yard maintenance. My goal is to help at least 10 households keep their yards looking great while gaining responsibility, experience, and spending money.

Education

Evergreen Middle School 2025–Present
Seventh Grade Student 3.8 GPA

Experience

Oscar's Lawn Care 2022–Present
Lawn Mower
I have mowed lawns and helped with basic yard work for neighbors and family members for three years. Built trust with repeat clients by being reliable and accountable.

Oscar's Smart-Start Tutoring 2021–Present
Math Tutor
Help younger students (grades 2–5) understand math concepts like addition, subtraction, multiplication, division, and fractions. Known for being patient and encouraging.

Volunteer Work

Vista House Breadbasket 2023–2024
Stock Boy/Organizer
Helped the Flint Hills Breadbasket organize food donations.

Skills

- Leadership
- Mathematics
- Customer Care
- Multitasking
- Time Management
- Problem-Solving

References

Paige Turner
Paige@reallygreatsite.com

Claudia Flowers
Claudia@reallygreatsite.com

Samir Grassy
Samir@reallygreatsite.com

Addie Up
Addie@reallygreatsite.com

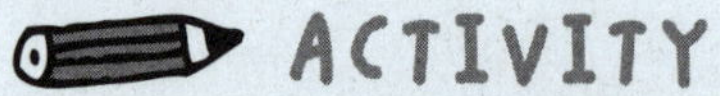

Land Your First Job

You've probably daydreamed about what you want to be when you grow up and what it'll feel like. No matter what career areas interest us, we all want a job we like. So, let's talk about how to focus your search and find the right job for you.

Part 1: Brainstorm

For this part, think of as many ideas as possible—even if they seem silly or unrealistic—and write them all down. Just let the ideas flow.

1. **Identify your strengths and interests.** Let these questions guide you:

   What are you good at? (*Examples: sports, art, writing, talking to others, playing violin, organizing, speaking a second language, caregiving, and so on*)

   ___

   ___

   What do you enjoy doing? (*Examples: making things, playing sports, singing, being with kids or animals, organizing events with friends, and so on*)

   ___

   ___

   What do people ask you for help with? (*Examples: homework, fixing things, learning a sport, yard chores, and so on*)

   ___

   ___

2. **Brainstorm possible jobs.** These questions can help you:

Who could use your help? (*Think about family, friends, neighbors, and classmates first. Is there a job you could do to help them?*)

____

____

What businesses are in your community? Name some places you'd be interested in working. (*Does anyone need help cleaning their office, delivering things, or assisting with an event? Maybe a local farmers' market? Or a day care center?*)

____

____

What do other kids your age do to make money? *(Talk to your friends, cousins, or older siblings.)*

____

____

Do you know any business owners in town? (*Maybe a family friend, your coach, a friend's parent or grandparent, a neighbor, someone from your church or synagogue?*)

____

____

Part 2: Prepare and Present

It's time to put all your brainstormed ideas to work for you!

1. **Create your résumé.** Take all the things you brainstormed in part 1, and put them into one place: your résumé. This is where you can highlight why you are a great candidate for the job you want. (Look back at page 20 for reminders on what a good résumé includes and looks like.) Design your own résumé, or go to a site like Canva.com for free résumé templates you can fill in with your information.
2. **Hit the pavement.** It's time to take action, and go after the job! Make copies of your résumé, and start talking to people who might hire you. Where are your potential customers or clients? You could start by knocking on doors (of people you know) in your neighborhood or calling family members to share what you do and how you can help—but before you do, read on for some tips!
3. **Practice your pitch.** It's good to practice what you want to communicate to potential customers so you can say it with confidence. Here's an example: *"Hi, my name is Anusha, and I'm 12 years old. I am great with pets and would love to walk dogs in the neighborhood this summer. I'm responsible and love animals! If you are interested, or know someone who might be, please give them my number or email"* (or a parent's contact information). You can practice your pitch in front of the mirror or with a trusted adult or sibling.

4. **Send a message.** You could also write a job request note or email that includes:
   - Your name and age
   - What you're offering to help with
   - Why you're good at it
   - How they can contact you

Finally, don't get discouraged if you hear "Not right now" or "We're not hiring." That happens! It doesn't mean you're not ready; it just means you might need to get a little creative.

Many jobs won't be available officially until you are 16 or older, but that doesn't mean you can't start building experience now. Here are two suggestions to keep moving forward and building your résumé:

1. **Volunteer in your area of interest.** If no one is hiring dog walkers in your neighborhood, you could still volunteer at the local pet shelter. Are you great at organizing? Perhaps you could offer to help with an upcoming school or church event.
2. **Keep track of all you are learning.** All the experience and knowledge you gather as a volunteer will help you in the future, and you can include it on your résumé. This way, when you apply for a job, you can show that you've already got experience.

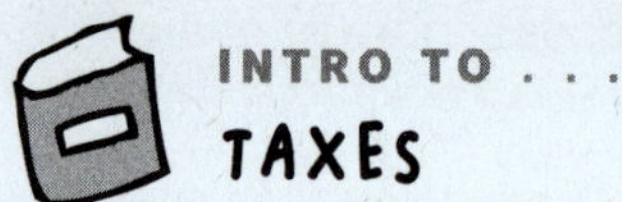

INTRO TO . . . TAXES

Taxes are an important part of what makes living in our communities possible. We all chip in by paying our fair share for the benefit of everyone.

Here's how it works: We all pay taxes on the money we earn, and the taxes go to our federal government, and in many cases, our state government (depending on your state). The government is like the "boss" of our state and country—it helps make rules, keep things fair, and take care of the stuff that everyone uses.

Every time we make money from a job or business, we pay a portion of that income in taxes. Taxes aren't a bad thing; they are just part of being in a community.

Here are some of the things taxes pay for:

- parks
- schools
- libraries
- fire departments
- sidewalks
- roads
- bridges
- services

Career Quest: Explore Your Future

Figuring out what you want to be when you grow up can be overwhelming because there are so many jobs to choose from. You may want to get a **job** as a babysitter now, but perhaps you'd like to have a **career** as a teacher. A career is a job that you have for a long time. You might do the same job for different businesses, but your career stays the same. For example, a banker might work at several different banks in their lifetime, but their career is being a banker.

Sometimes, people change careers as their interests and skills change and grow. Do you know what career *you* might enjoy? Let's dive into this career quest to get some ideas!

1. The first stop on our career quest is **SKILLVILLE**. Check off all the skills that apply to you, then describe exactly what you're good at (looking back at your brainstorm from page 22 if needed):

   - ☐ Making things

     ____

   - ☐ Helping people

     ____

   - ☐ Playing sports or instruments

     ____

   - ☐ Math, writing, language, spelling, speaking

     ____

- [ ] Organizing (events, spaces, activities, and more)

____

- [ ] Other

____

2. Here we are, at **INTEREST ISLAND**. What are your interests? What do you love to do?

- [ ] Play with animals
- [ ] Play with children
- [ ] Build things
- [ ] Make art or music
- [ ] Science
- [ ] Sports
- [ ] Writing
- [ ] Technology
- [ ] Video games
- [ ] Other

____

____

____

____

____

____

3. Our next stop is **VALUE VALLEY**. The work you do should make you feel good and match your **values**. A value is a character trait that's important to you and who you are. Check off any values that are important to you, then list any others that apply to you:

- ☐ Creativity
- ☐ Independence
- ☐ Leadership
- ☐ Honesty
- ☐ Kindness
- ☐ Generosity
- ☐ Responsibility
- ☐ Fairness
- ☐ Happiness
- ☐ Humor
- ☐ Other
- ☐ Health
- ☐ Nature and conservation
- ☐ Spirituality
- ☐ Patriotism
- ☐ Teamwork
- ☐ Family
- ☐ Civic-mindedness (making a difference in your community)

____

____

____

____

____

____

4. Now, let's get to our final destination—**YOUR CAREER!** Look at everything you wrote in Skillville, Interest Island, and Value Valley. Can you think of any jobs that combine your skills, interests, and values? List them here.

____

____

____

____

____

____

____

____

CHAPTER 2

BANK IT RIGHT

Learning About Checking and Savings

It's important to understand banking and savings accounts because you'll need to use them to manage your money throughout your whole life. In fact, learning how to manage money now will give you a big head start in being able to manage money well as an adult.

Find the Right Bank

As a young kid, you may have just associated the bank with a boring grown-up errand. But now that we're talking about your money, it's your turn to be the customer. Sure, you can keep your money in a wallet or a safe, but by putting it in a bank account instead, you can earn **interest**. *Interest* is a payment the bank offers you for keeping your money there.

Additionally, banks are a safe place to put your money. They are protected by a government agency called the Federal Deposit Insurance Corporation (FDIC), so if anything ever happened to your bank, like it closed or burned down, your money would still be safe.

So, how do you choose which bank to use? There are a few things to consider:

- **Access:** Make sure the funds in your bank account are easy to access when you need them. The bank's website and app should be easy to use and understand. If you need to go to the bank, you'll want them to have locations near you.
- **Fees:** Make sure you know whether there are any fees for keeping your money in the bank. Some banks charge fees if you don't keep a certain amount of money there. Other banks charge monthly fees just for using their bank. So, look for a bank account with no monthly fees or minimum amount requirements.
- **Benefits:** Does the bank have kid-friendly accounts? Pay a high amount of interest? Offer cool tools you can use to save more?
- **Safety:** Double-check that your bank is protected by the FDIC.

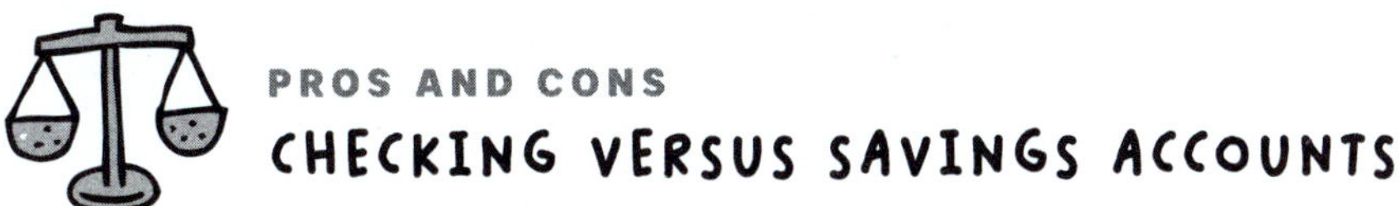

PROS AND CONS

CHECKING VERSUS SAVINGS ACCOUNTS

The two main types of accounts most kids set up are **checking** and **savings**. A checking account is where you keep money you are going to spend soon, such as on groceries, entertainment, or bills. A savings account is where you keep money you want to save for use in the future. You might keep money here that you are saving for a bike, a computer, concert tickets, or surprise expenses.

Most adults have both a checking and a savings account. As a kid, you might start out with a savings account first. It can be a safe place to keep your allowance, gifts of money you receive, or money you earn from jobs. Plus, some savings accounts earn interest. We'll talk about this more on page 56. It also makes your money a little less accessible than keeping it all in your wallet, where you might be tempted to spend it too quickly!

Break Down Bank Statements

Shohei opened a bank account last month, and he received his first **statement** this week. A *statement* is like a summary of all that happens in your account each month. Here's what it includes:

- **Starting balance:** This is the amount of money in your account at the beginning of the month or banking cycle.
- **Deposits:** This is all the money that came into your account during the month, such as money you put in from your allowance or job earnings.
- **Withdrawals:** This is the money that came out of your account during the month. This would include anything you spent money on that month.
- **Ending balance:** This is the amount of money your account contained on the last day of the month or banking cycle, which takes into account any deposits or withdrawals.

Monthly Statement

ABC Bank
123-456-7890
123 Anywhere St., Any City

Milton Pup
123-456-7890
123 Anywhere St., Any City, ST 12345

July 30, 2025

BEGINNING BALANCE July 1, 2025 **$5,123.27**

DEPOSITS

Check Deposit	$160.00
Electronic Deposit	$530.17

WITHDRAWALS

Dog Treat Subscription	$50.00
Grocery	$136.98
Pet Store	$23.45

ENDING BALANCE July 30, 2025 **$5,603.01**

Shohei didn't really know why this statement was important, so he tossed it aside. Later, he sat down with his mom, who explained why it's good to review the statement:

- It's important to review the withdrawals to make sure they're correct. For example, if you see the same amount charged twice by the same store, you'll need to make sure they didn't accidentally charge you double.
- Likewise, you want to make sure you got credited for all your deposits.
- You can see how much you spend each month and what you spend it on. This can help you figure out where you spend most of your money and where you can cut costs.
- You can also determine whether you have extra money each month that you could save or invest (we'll talk about that soon!).

Access Your Cash

Money that you keep in a bank account can be accessed in a few different ways:

- **Cash withdrawal:** You can go to the bank and ask to take some money out of your account in cash. You'll need to either write a check or fill out a withdrawal form with your account number on it. You may also need to bring identification or have a parent with you, depending on your bank.
- **Debit card:** This card is linked to your bank account and can be used at a store or online to buy something. When you use the card to pay for something, the money is automatically taken out of your account, so you don't have to get physical cash to pay for the item.
- **ATM withdrawal:** Banks have ATMs (automated teller machines), which are machines containing money you can withdraw if you have a debit card connected to your account. At an ATM, you insert the debit card, enter your PIN (personal identification number, which is a code that only you know), type in the requested amount, and the machine gives you the cash.
- **Venmo, PayPal, Apple Pay, for example:** These are just a few apps that let you pay for things electronically or send money to a person from your bank account. These services take the money from your account and send it to someone else. For example, if you're with your friends and one person buys a pizza to share, everyone else can send them money to pay for their portion.

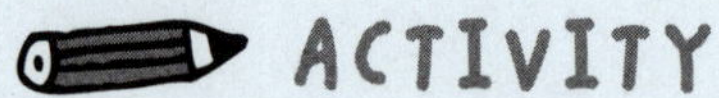

Banking Beginnings: Your First Bank Account

Are you ready to take your money game to the next level? In this section, we'll walk through the four easy steps for opening your bank account. Let's get started, with a head-to-head bank competition!

1. **Choose the right bank for you.** Start by doing an online investigation and compare two banks, using the chart on the next page.
2. **Gather your information.** To open an account, you need proof of who you are. You usually need to have your social security number, birth date, and a parent or guardian with you.
3. **Open the account at the bank you chose or online.** Whether you open your account at the bank or on their website, you will be asked for the information you gathered in step 2. Be sure to have a parent or guardian with you to do this.
4. **Make your first deposit.** Once the account is set up, you can deposit money in it to start saving!

HEAD-TO-HEAD MATCHUP

BANK 1 VERSUS **BANK 2**

______________________ ______________________

BANK 1

ACCESS

- ☐ Money easy to get
- ☐ Locations near me
- ☐ Easy-to-use website

FEES

- ☐ No monthly fees
- ☐ No minimum balance

BENEFITS

- ☐ Kid-friendly accounts
- ☐ Cool tools/perks
- ☐ Interest rate ________
- ☐ FDIC insured

BANK 2

ACCESS

- ☐ Money easy to get
- ☐ Locations near me
- ☐ Easy-to-use website

FEES

- ☐ No monthly fees
- ☐ No minimum balance

BENEFITS

- ☐ Kid-friendly accounts
- ☐ Cool tools/perks
- ☐ Interest rate ________
- ☐ FDIC insured

AND THE WINNER IS ______________________________!

PART TWO

MAPPING YOUR MILLIONAIRE PATH

CHAPTER 3

BUDGET BASICS

Creating a Plan for Your Money

Budgeting means figuring out how much money comes in and goes out every month, so how much you earn versus how much you spend. Having a **budget**, or a specific spending and saving plan, can be a great way to handle your money well. In this chapter, you will discover your spending style, consider needs versus wants, and learn how to create a budget like a pro.

Discover Your Spending Style

Have you ever wondered what your money habits say about you? Are you someone who likes to spend money right away, save every penny, or think things through before buying? This quick quiz will help you figure out your spending style. Just circle the answers that sound most like you, and see which money personality you match with.

1. You see a pair of shoes you just ***have*** to have. What do you do?
   a. Can't wait—buy them now!
   b. Do some research to see if I can get a better deal or find a coupon.
   c. Make a savings plan, and think about it for a while.

2. You get a $50 gift card for your birthday. What do you do?
   a. Head to the store to spend it.
   b. Think about what I've been wanting, and consider my options.
   c. Save it for something big down the road.

3. The coolest new skin came out in Fortnite, or you see a new gadget at the store that everyone is talking about. What's your next move?
   a. Buy it now so I don't miss out!
   b. Wait a bit to read the reviews, and ask friends if it's worth it.
   c. Pass on buying it, unless it's something I have been waiting for.

4. How do you feel after spending money?
   a. Excited! It's fun to get new stuff.
   b. Pretty good if I know I made a good choice.
   c. A little uncertain. Should I have saved that money instead?

5. When you plan a day out with friends, how do you plan for the cost?
   a. I don't really think about the cost; I just figure it out as I go.
   b. I bring enough money for what I think I'll need and set a spending limit for myself.
   c. I try to spend as little as possible or skip things that cost too much.

How'd you do? Here is your spending style based on your answers:

If your answers were all or mostly A's—the **Speedy Spender**. You love spending money the minute it's in your grasp. Whether it's the newest game or a cool hoodie you saw at the store, you just *have to* have it now. Being excited about your money is fun, but sometimes a little planning can help you get more for your buck.

If your answers were all or mostly B's—the **Savvy Spender**. You're a money expert in the making! You think before you buy, check for better deals, and know when it's worth spending or better to wait. You strike a good balance between enjoying your money now and saving it for later.

If your answers were all or mostly C's—the **Super Saver**. You are great at holding on to your money and thinking things through. You might wait a long time before making a purchase or even be hesitant to spend at all. Saving is an excellent skill, but keep in mind that it's okay to have fun with money sometimes, too.

Sorting Needs Versus Wants

Making smart choices with your money starts with recognizing the difference between needs and wants. In this scenario, you'll learn how to sort one from the other so you can create a savvy shopping plan that helps you spend wisely while still accomplishing your goals.

Mavis is heading into a new school year, and her parents have given her a budget of $300 for school clothes. She needs a few basics to start the year: a pair of shoes, two pairs of pants, a few shirts, and maybe a dress or two.

While shopping, Mavis finds a pair of designer shoes she wants for $150. They are supercool and all the older girls are wearing them. But she knows that if she spends half her budget on just the shoes, she won't have money much left for the other items.

She also sees a pair of nice, comfy shoes that she likes for $60—not as cool, but still cute. If she chooses the more affordable shoes, she'll be able to buy more outfit options.

What should Mavis do?

Let's help her make a smart shopping plan:

1. What are Mavis's needs versus her wants?

   Needs:

   ____

   Wants:

   ____

2. If Mavis buys the $150 shoes, do you think she'll be able to afford everything else on her list with the remainder of her money?

____

____

3. What are the pros and cons of buying the less-expensive shoes?

Pros:

____

Cons:

____

4. If you were Mavis, what would you do, and why?

____

____

Yep, managing money comes with a lot of decisions and trade-offs. There's not always a right or wrong way to do it, just as long as you find a balance that lets you get all of your needs met while still leaving you a little for the wants, too!

INTRO TO . . .

50/30/20 RULE . . . AND A FEW OTHERS

Want a simple way to manage your money? In this section, you'll learn about a few different budgeting rules.

Let's start with the **50/30/20 budgeting rule**, a smart method that divides your spending into needs, wants, and savings. It's an easy way to stay on track, make smart choices, and feel more in control of your money.

How do you know how much of your income you can spend? A good guideline to use when building a budget is the 50/30/20 rule. This includes setting aside:

- **50 percent of your money for needs:** It's smart to set aside half of your budget for things you have to pay for regularly, like bills, rent, and food. Your parents might be paying for most of this now, but it's important to know for the future.
- **30 percent for wants:** These are the purchases you don't need, but want and could include expensive shoes, going to the movies, eating out, or a fun trip.
- **20 percent for savings:** It's good to get into the habit of saving at least 20 percent of your income every time you get paid. Some of that savings should be for the future and some for emergency expenses.

Let's look at an example: Carlos made $1,200 mowing lawns this month and wants to use the 50/30/20 rule. How much would go toward each category?

50 percent needs	**30 percent wants**	**20 percent savings**
= $600	= $360	= $240

GIVE/SAVE/SPEND RULE

Okay, now that you're familiar with 50/30/20, here's some good news: Chances are, you're not responsible for paying much, if anything, toward your family's household expenses. This means you have a higher percentage of disposable (available) income now than you may ever have again!

In this case, the 50/30/20 rule isn't necessary. A better ratio for this time of life when you have fewer financial obligations might be something like 10/20/70, where you designate 10 percent to giving (donating to a cause you believe in), 20 percent to savings, and the remainder to spending.

This ratio is pretty flexible, depending on your spending style and long-term goals. If you're a saver, you may choose to adjust this ratio to 10/40/60 or an even higher savings level. Just make sure you:

- Consistently set aside money for each category
- Are realistic about the ratio you choose so you don't make a habit of tapping into savings
- Think about how you can use this time to set yourself up for the financial future you want—before all the adult responsibilities roll in

One more thing: If you're curious about why it's important to put some of your money toward giving to others, here's why. Giving:

- Sets you up to be mindful of other people's needs
- Builds positive character traits and values
- Connects you with the community and world around you
- Creates a sense of social responsibility
- Increases your sense of gratitude
- Makes the world a better place!

Building Your First Budget

Making a budget is like making a plan for your money to decide where it will go. Having a budget puts *you* in charge of your money, not the other way around.

Let's create a budget together!

1. At the top of your budget sheet is where you list your **income** sources—money that comes *in* each month. This could include money earned from working, allowance, tutoring, gifts, and other things. Then, add up all these income sources to get your total monthly income.
2. Next, plan for the month's **expenses**, money that goes *out*. These might include buying toys, games, snacks, clothes, crafts, manicures, books, gifts, sports gear, or fun outings, making charitable donations, and savings. Add these up to determine your monthly expenses.
3. Finally, subtract your total expenses from your total income. This is your monthly income after expenses. Using the examples in this chart, you subtract $225 in expenses from $300 in income, leaving you with $75 in monthly income after expenses.
4. Now, fill in the chart with your budget, and do the math!

Monthly Income (EXPECTED)		
	(Example: babysitting)	*$300*
Total Monthly Income		**$**

Monthly Expenses (EXPECTED)		
	(Example: savings)	*$200*
	(Example: candy)	*$25*
Total Monthly Expenses		**$**
Monthly Income Less Expenses		**$**

A budget can be tricky, as it might change from time to time. For example, you might have more babysitting gigs this month than last month, so you have more money to budget. Or, you might make a large purchase or have an emergency expense this month. Or maybe it's raining, and you can't mow the lawns you expected to, so you have less money than you expected. Either way, it's good to make an "expected" budget, but then track the "actual" income and expenses you had. You can use that information in your future budget. Let's look at an example:

The goal each month is to have a little bit left over after expenses. You can use those extra dollars to beef up your savings.

EXPECTED

Monthly Income	
Babysitting	$300
Lawn mowing	$200
Allowance	$100
Total Monthly Income	**$600**
Monthly Expenses	
Savings	$60
V-Bucks	$30
Candy	$15
Clothing	$100
Baseball tournament shirt	$45
Trip to the arcade	$60
Pokémon cards	$30
Movies with friends	$25
LED lights for bedroom	$50
Total Monthly Expenses	**$415**
Monthly Income Less Expenses	**$185**

ACTUAL

Monthly Income	
Babysitting	$330
Lawn mowing	$150
Allowance	$100
Total Monthly Income	**$580**
Monthly Expenses	
Savings	$60
V-Bucks	$35
Candy	$36
Clothing	$109
Baseball tournament shirt	$45
Trip to the arcade	$60
Pokémon cards	$30
Movies with friends	$25
LED lights for bedroom	$65
Gift for Mother's Day	$55
Replacing broken headphones	$30
Total Monthly Expenses	**$550**
Monthly Income Less Expenses	**$30**

CHAPTER 4

THE ART OF SAVING

Turning Small Steps into Big Gains

Saving money might not sound very exciting—after all, it's just sitting there, waiting to be spent! But in reality, saving is one of the most powerful habits you can build. When you save a little every time you get money from allowance, for your birthday, or a job, you're giving your future self the gift of more choices and freedom. Start strengthening your saving muscles now, and by the time you're an adult, you'll be a money management pro.

Smart Saving Methods

There's no one-size-fits-all way of saving—everyone has their own way. Finding the method that works for you can make a big difference in your success. In this section, we'll explore some common savings strategies. All of them can help you build better habits, reach your goals faster, and feel confident about your financial future. Here are a few methods to try:

1. Pay yourself first.
    - ➔ As soon as you get money, set aside a chunk for savings before you spend any of it.
    - ➔ Save 10 to 20 percent every time you make money.

2. Set a savings goal.

   - Got your eye on something you want to save for? Maybe some earrings, a bicycle, or a special trip?
   - Decide how much the item will cost, and start making a savings plan to get there.
   - Use the following "savings tracker" or download a savings tracker app (see page 131) to track your progress toward your goal.

3. Use the Give/Save/Spend rule (see page 48).

   - This is a great way to help others, save, and still have fun spending.
   - Every time you get paid, some of it goes to giving, some gets put into savings, and the rest can be spent.
   - You choose how much of each paycheck goes into each bucket. One good guideline is 5 to 10 percent to giving, 10 to 20 percent for savings, and the remainder to spending.

4. Use the 50/30/20 rule (see page 47).

   - This is a good budgeting method for people who contribute to household expenses.
   - With this method, 50 percent goes to needs, 30 percent to wants, and 20 percent to savings.

When you find the method that works best for you, make it a habit. Consistency is the key to good money management!

MONTHLY SAVINGS TRACKER

	WEEK 1	WEEK 2	WEEK 3	WEEK 4
JANUARY	$	$	$	$
FEBRUARY	$	$	$	$
MARCH	$	$	$	$
APRIL	$	$	$	$
MAY	$	$	$	$
JUNE	$	$	$	$
JULY	$	$	$	$
AUGUST	$	$	$	$
SEPTEMBER	$	$	$	$
OCTOBER	$	$	$	$
NOVEMBER	$	$	$	$
DECEMBER	$	$	$	$

GOAL: $ ____________

SAVING FOR: ____

INTRO TO . . . INTEREST

Saving money can pay off. A bank may pay you interest for keeping money in your account. For example, if your savings account pays 1 percent and you put in $1,000, after a year the bank adds $10.

Math: $1,000 × 0.01 = $10.

But interest can also work against you when you borrow. Say you buy a Nintendo Switch for $300 on a credit card. If you don't pay it off that month, the company charges interest every month you carry a balance. Credit card interest is much higher—often 24 percent or more—so you end up paying more than the Switch actually cost.

Tip: When multiplying with a percent, move the decimal two spaces left.
Example: 25 percent = 0.25

Save Now, Enjoy Later

Zeke is getting into the smart habit of saving every time he gets paid. He has decided to save 15 percent of all the income he receives from dog walking, tutoring younger kids in math, and his allowance from his parents.

Here's a breakdown of how much money Zeke earns and saves each month:

Income Savings			
Monthly Income Sources	**Monthly Income**		**15 Percent to Savings**
Dog walking	$600		$90
Tutoring	$400		$60
Allowance	$30		$5
Total Monthly Income	**$1,030**	**Total Monthly Savings**	**$155**

Zeke is consistently saving $155 per month. If he does this for the entire year, he will end up with $1,860 in savings. But if the bank pays interest, he'll have even more in his account.

Let's say the bank pays 1 percent interest. If the interest is **compounded** monthly, Zeke will earn about $10 in interest over the course of the year. So, at the end of the year, his bank account balance would actually be around $1,870. You may be asking, *What does compounded mean?* Read on!

Understanding Simple Versus Compound Interest

Interest comes in two forms: simple and compound.

Simple interest means you earn a **flat** (unchanging) rate on the money you deposit. If the rate is 5 percent and you put in $100, you earn $5 each year.

Compound interest means you earn not only on your deposit but also on the interest already earned—interest on interest! With $100 at 5 percent compound interest, you earn $5 the first year. In year two, you now have $105, so you earn 5 percent on *that*, which is $5.25. It may not seem like much at first, but the interest keeps growing each year as your account grows.

Let's test this out!

1. Grab two jars or glasses and a bowl full of small items (such as Skittles, pennies, or marbles).
2. Set the jars side by side, and place one item in each jar.
3. Next, place one item in the left jar, but put two in the right jar.
4. Next, place one item in the left jar, but put three in the right jar.
5. Continue increasing the number of items in the right jar until the bowl is empty.

That's the idea behind compound interest. Compound interest means that your interest is getting interest, and this adds up over time, especially as your money grows.

INTRO TO . . .

INVESTMENTS: GROWTH AND DECLINE

Investments go up and down in the short run (daily, weekly, monthly), but over a longer time period (years and decades) your money will grow much faster in investments than in savings accounts. Here's an example:

You bought one share of Amazon stock in July 2015 for about $35. The stock price moves (up or down) based on what is going on with that company at that moment. If the company is doing well, the stock price might be higher today than it was yesterday. If some bad news came out, it might drop suddenly.

Fast-forward to July 2025, 10 years later: That same Amazon share would be worth around $185. That's more than five times what you paid to buy it!

So, even though stock prices go up and down along the way, over time, they typically go up, and sometimes a lot!

To compare: If you put that $35 into a savings account earning 1 percent interest, after 10 years it would be worth only $38.66.

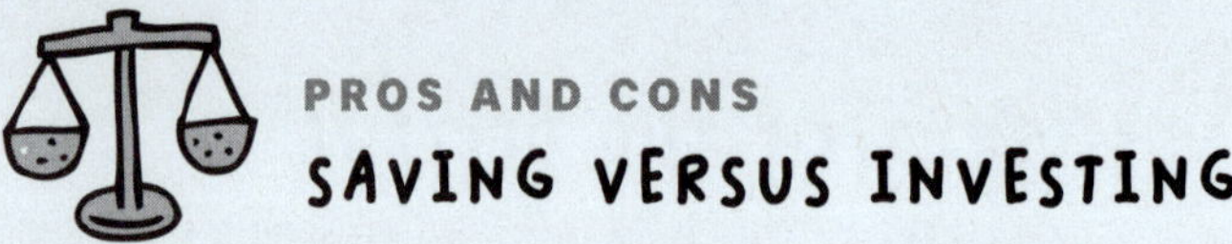

PROS AND CONS

SAVING VERSUS INVESTING

Saving is a great place to start, but if you want to earn even more from your money, you'll want to **invest** it.

Investing means putting your money into something that it can grow with over time. Investments are riskier than savings accounts, meaning the value can go up or down, but over the long term, investments can make you a lot more money than a savings account.

SAVINGS ACCOUNT PROS AND CONS

PROS

- It's safe. Your money stays in the savings account.
- It's easy to access your money any time you need it.

CONS

- Not much growth happens, and you can actually lose money to inflation over time. Inflation is when the cost of goods and services increases, reducing the purchasing power of your money. Think about it this way: If you're only earning 1 percent interest and inflation goes up 3 percent, your money isn't growing at the same rate you need for spending.
- If you only save and don't invest, you might not be able to reach your big goals in the future.

INVESTING PROS AND CONS

PROS

- Your money has a better chance to grow over time (see chapter 9 for more on this).
- Investing over a long period of time can help you reach very big goals in the future (see part three).

CONS

- Investing comes with risks. Investment values move up and down, like a roller coaster, but over time you'll likely end up with more money (as in the Amazon example on page 59).
- You usually have to leave your money alone in the investment for a long time—often decades. Building wealth takes time.

HERE'S THE BIG PICTURE

- Saving is like putting money into a piggy bank. It's safe but slow to grow.
- Investing is like planting a "money tree": riskier, but grows bigger over time if you're patient and keep adding.
- You need both: savings for stability now, investments for growth in the future.

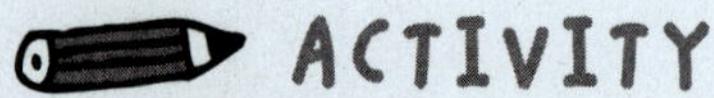

Inflation Tracker

Have you ever heard an adult talk about how much things cost when they were kids? Well, it may surprise you, too, to see how inflation has increased prices even since you were born.

1. Go to the grocery store or look on the store's app. How much does a gallon of milk cost today?

   ____

2. Next, search online for what a gallon of milk cost the year you were born.

   ____

3. What's the difference—how much did the cost go up?

   ____

4. Take a guess what a gallon of milk will cost 10 years from now.

   ____

If you'd like, repeat this activity with a loaf of bread, a dozen eggs, your favorite car, concert tickets—whatever grabs your curiosity!

Watch Your Savings Grow

Shante is making great money babysitting—everyone wants to hire her! If she puts $300 per month in a savings account that earns 2 percent compound interest, how much money would she have saved in a year? Let's find out!

- ➔ **Deposit:** $300 per month
- ➔ **Interest:** 2 percent compounded per year = 0.02 percent annually
- ➔ **Monthly interest rate** = 0.02 divided by 12 = 0.0016667 per month

Month	Deposit	Total Interest Earned	Total Balance
January	$300.00	$0.50	$300.50
February	$300.00	$1.00	$601.50
March	$300.00	$1.50	$903.00
April	$300.00	$2.01	$1,205.01
May	$300.00	$2.51	$1,507.52
June	$300.00	$3.01	$1,810.53
July	$300.00	$3.52	$2,114.05
August	$300.00	$4.02	$2,418.07
September	$300.00	$4.53	$2,722.60
October	$300.00	$5.04	$3,027.64
November	$300.00	$5.55	$3,333.19
December	$300.00	$6.06	$3,639.25

Did you notice? The amount of interest Shante earned grew each month because her balance kept getting higher and she was gaining compounded interest . . . interest on her deposits plus her earned interest.

CHAPTER 5

SPENDING SMART

How to Find Deals, Spot Value, and Dodge Scams

Spending money involves a whole lot of choices and decisions, and there are a lot of tempting options out there! It's important to look for good deals, get good value, and watch out for scams. Making wise choices consistently is how you become a smart spender.

Becoming a Bargain Hunter

There are lots of ways to save money when shopping. Here are a few ideas to become a true bargain hunter:

- **Compare prices:** Before buying something, check other stores or websites to see if you can get it for a better price.
- **Buy used:** Often, you can find secondhand stuff for a fraction of the price of new. Buying used can make good sense for things like sporting gear, bicycles, clothes, and toys. Check online sales sites, garage sales, thrift stores, or resale sites like eBay.

- **Wait for a sale:** If the item you want is full price, there's a chance it will, eventually, go on sale. Sometimes, just by waiting a week or two, the price will come down. It's also good to plan big purchases around holiday sales, like Black Friday, end of season, or Memorial Day. You can also try out some price-tracking apps or websites.
- **Use coupons and discount codes:** Store coupons can often be found on the company's website. Sometimes, you can get a discount by signing up for a company's mailing list. Other times, coupons come by mail. You can also check coupon sites like Retailmenot.com to see if your desired store has a coupon code available.

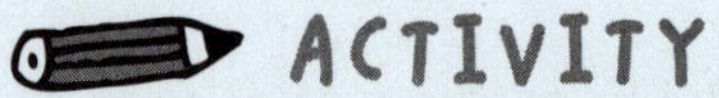

Avoiding Marketing Tricks and Impulse Buys

Advertisements are *everywhere*, trying to convince you to buy things even when you don't need them. By learning how to spot common marketing tricks, you can make smarter choices with your money, and avoid **impulse buys**, which are purchases you make and things you buy quickly without really thinking them through. Here are some common tricks that marketers use:

Impulse zones

Ever notice that there are always fun gadgets, toys, and candy to look at as you're waiting in the checkout line? This is no accident! Stores want to tempt you to grab these things and throw them on the counter with your other purchases.

Avoid the trap! Ask yourself, *Do I need this, or is it just something I want because it's right here?*

Can you think of a time you've been tempted by an impulse zone? What did you do?

____

____

"Free" gifts

Ever hear, "Act now, and we'll also send you this free gift!"? Marketers sometimes offer a "free" gift when you buy something, but the item you're buying is actually priced higher than it should be to cover the cost of the "free" gift.

Avoid the trap! Ask yourself, *Is this gift really free or am I paying for it? And is it worth it?*

Can you think of a time you've been tempted by a free gift? Was it really a good value?

____

____

Celebrity value

Marketers often show celebrities, or people you admire, using a product to try to get you to buy it.

Avoid the trap! Just because something is popular, or your favorite celebrity likes it, doesn't mean it's a good product, or something you need.

Have you bought something because someone you admired was using it? Did you really need it?

____

____

Subscription trap

Kids and adults sign up for a "free trial" of something, but then it turns into an ongoing paid subscription that's hard to turn off. And they don't send you reminders, so you may keep paying for a subscription you've forgotten about and don't even use!

Avoid the trap! Ask yourself, *Do I really need this subscription? Is it worth the hassle to cancel later?* (If you do opt for a free trial, set a calendar reminder before the trial ends to evaluate whether to continue with it!)

Have you ever accepted a free trial, then ended up paying for it or forgetting about it? If so, what was it?

___

___

Limited-time offers

Ads might say something is "available only for a limited time," "limited-time offer for this price," or a "limited drop," making it seem urgent to buy it now. This is just a trick to get you to act quickly.

Avoid the trap! Ask yourself, *Is this price really for a limited time, or are they just trying to get me to buy it today?*

Have you ever felt like you needed to buy something before "time ran out"? What did you do, and how did you feel about your decision?

___

___

Scarcity trap

Marketers might use the terms "While supplies last!" or "Only a few left!" This tactic is designed to get you to act fast, without thinking through your purchase.

Avoid the trap! If you weren't already planning to buy the item, wait until you're ready. You may change your mind about the purchase in the meantime, and the price may even go down!

Have you ever felt like you needed to buy something before it sold out? What happened? Did it sell out? Did it ever return?

____

____

What are some other marketing and sales tricks you've seen?

Write them here. *Example: Brightly colored packaging*

____

____

____

What strategies can you use to avoid these marketing scams? *Example: If I find something I want to buy that I wasn't planning to buy, I'll wait 24 hours before I make the purchase.*

____

____

____

INTRO TO . . . SCAMS

Money scams can happen to anyone—whether you're a kid or adult! Here are some common scams to look out for:

FAKE PRIZES OR GIVEAWAYS

You get a message or see an ad saying that you "won a prize"—but you just have to pay a small fee or give your personal information (like your address, bank information, birthday, or social security number) to receive it.

→ **Here's the truth!** Real prizes don't require you to pay or give personal information to win. Scammers will do anything to get your personal information.

GIFT CARD SCAMS

A scammer asks you for payment for something fake in the form of a gift card.

→ **Here's the truth!** Never buy gift cards for someone you don't know personally—it's a scam. Real companies never ask for payment in the form of gift cards.

PHISHING EMAILS, TEXTS, OR MESSAGES

You get an email saying it's from your school, your friend, or your favorite game or store. They ask you to click a link or share a password.

→ **Here's the truth!** This kind of message is sent for illegal reasons, such as to install a virus on your device or steal your identity. Never click on a link in a text or email if you don't know for sure where it's coming from. Look at the actual email address for a clue—even though the sender might say your friend's name, the email address might be completely different. And never give out your personal information without checking with your adult first.

DEBIT CARD THEFT

You're at a friend's house for a sleepover, and you leave your wallet on the counter. The next day, you see a charge on your card for a food delivery you didn't order. One of the other kids helped themselves to your card!

➜ **Here's the truth!** Debit cards are convenient, but they can be used easily by others. Never let your debit card out of your sight. Keep it on you or in a safe place where nobody can see it. It's even risky to let a restaurant server or store employee walk away with your card to process your payment. All someone needs to do is snap a picture of your card, and then they have your card number and can make purchases with your money. If you think it's been used without your knowledge, call your bank right away so they can freeze or cancel that card and issue you a new one. You can also dispute the charge with the merchant or the bank to try to get a refund.

FAKE ONLINE STORES

A new website is listing cool things for really low prices. This seems like a great deal, so you buy something, but you never receive it!

➜ **Here's the truth!** Anyone can create a website—even a scammer. Always double-check that a website or business is real before buying anything there. Check its reviews on Trustpilot.com to make sure it's legit and reliable. If the reviews are under 3.5, you should probably find another place to buy your item.

ONLINE GAMING SCAMS

You're always being offered "free" game coins, skins, upgrades, or cheats, but they want your personal information or payment first. What should you do?

→ **Here's the truth!** You're dealing with a scammer. If it sounds too good to be true, it probably is. If you want upgrades, purchase these virtual items directly using a gaming gift card like Xbox, V-Bucks, or Robux.

IMPERSONATORS

You get an urgent phone call from a friend asking for money. "I lost my phone," they say. "Send money quick!" It sounds like them, but seems weird that they are calling you with this request.

→ **Here's the truth!** Scammers like to use this trick with older people, pretending they're a grandchild in a scary situation. They even sound like the person! They may also set up fake social media accounts in the name of people you like and follow. When this happens, they may message you, sending scam links or asking for information. Always double-check that the person you are talking to or interacting with is who they say they are, especially if they are asking you for something.

Shop Smart for Big-Ticket Items

Buying a big-ticket "dream item" like concert tickets, a bicycle, laptop, or car can take a while to save up for and might require some planning. Where to start?

- Figure out how much the item will cost.
- Estimate how long it will take you to save for it, based on your income sources and other expenses.
- Strategize. If you want to speed up the time it takes to save enough for your purchase, how can you earn more money between now and then?

Here's a worksheet to help guide you.

BIG-TICKET ITEM SAVINGS GOAL WORKSHEET

Name ______________________________

Today's date ______________________________

My dream item ______________________________

Why I want it ______________________________

Cost $ ______________________

How much money I have $ ______________________

How much more I need to save $ ______________________

My Savings Plan

I will save ____________ every week.

I hope to reach my goal by ________ / ________ / ________ .

Ways I can earn or save money

____

____

____

____

Good Value Versus Good Deals

Just because something costs less doesn't mean it's the best choice. A good **deal** (low price) and good **value** (good product for the money) aren't always the same thing. In this activity, you'll answer smart questions to help you decide if a purchase is truly worth it. Let's learn how to spot real value, not just low prices!

Name an item that you would like to save for.

____

Where can you buy this item? List at least two places/sites where you can buy it, and how much it costs at each one:

____

____

____

____

Which is the best deal? Are you sacrificing anything by paying the lower price? Before you answer this question:

- **Check the quality:** Is the item made well? Will it last a long time? Read the reviews and buy from trusted brands.
- **Compare prices:** Does this item have a different cost at other stores or websites? If the price is too cheap, it might be a fake. Can you buy this item used and still get good value out of it?

- **Think about usefulness:** How often will you use this item? An expensive item that you get a lot of use out of is actually a better deal than a cheap product that you never use or that breaks quickly.

Moral of the story: A good deal is getting something that works well, lasts long, and makes you happy—not just something that's cheap!

CHAPTER 6

CREDIT UNCOVERED

Understanding Scores, Reports, and History

When adults borrow money (like with a credit card or loan), they build a credit score—a report card for how well they pay back borrowed money. A good score shows lenders you can be trusted and helps you get better deals.

Understanding Credit

A credit score shows how well a person manages money and debt. It's based on:

- Making payments on time
- How long it takes to pay back money
- How much total debt they have

A good credit score helps adults:

- Borrow money for a house, business, or car
- Pay less in interest and fees
- Get approved faster for things like renting an apartment or college loans

Decode a Credit Report

Brandon wants to build his credit. He's had a credit card for a few years, usually pays on time (with a few late payments), has a $1,000 limit, and owes $800—so he's paying lots of interest. Now he wants to buy his first car and borrow money but doesn't know anything about his credit report. Let's get Brandon up to speed!

A credit report shows personal information and your credit history. Lenders can see:

- **Your personal information:** Basic details to confirm your identity. Always check this—people with the same name or scammers could cause mistakes.
- **Accounts:** All the places you've borrowed money (credit cards, car loans, student loans, mortgages) and what you owe.
- **Payment history:** Whether you pay on time and **in full**, or if you've made late payments.
- **Credit inquiries:** How many times you've applied for credit. Lenders check your report each time you apply for a loan or card.

When using credit, there's a limit on how much you can use. For example, a new credit card might have a $500 limit (Brandon's is $1,000). That means you have $500 of credit available. If you use it all quickly, creditors may think you spend too much and be hesitant to give you more. But if you use only a small amount and pay it back on time, they may trust you with more credit later.

A healthy credit report shows on-time payments, no missed bills, and borrowing only what you can handle. Here's a snapshot of good vs. bad credit:

THINGS THAT HELP YOUR CREDIT SCORE	THINGS THAT HURT YOUR CREDIT SCORE
✓ Making payments on time	✕ Not having a credit history
✓ Keeping debt balances low	✕ Applying for credit often
✓ Paying off your credit card in full each month	✕ Making a late payment
	✕ Missing a payment
	✕ Paying less than the amount due
	✕ Borrowing more than you can pay back

Because of his late payments and high credit card balance, Brandon couldn't get a loan on his own. But the bank agreed to lend him money with a cosigner. A cosigner agrees to pay the debt if the borrower can't. Brandon's mother cosigned, trusting him to pay. Now, knowing how to protect his credit, Brandon pays his car loan on time each month and hasn't missed a single payment!

Credit Score Influencers

Now that you know what a credit score is, let's look at the key factors that influence it and why they matter. Understanding these helps you make smart choices and build a strong score over time.

Here are the top five factors that affect your credit score, in order of importance:

1. **Payment history**

   (most important—about ***35 percent*** *of your total score)*

   This shows you can be trusted to borrow money in the future.

   ➔ Do you pay your bills on time?

2. **Credit utilization/amount owed**

   *(important—****30 percent*** *of your total score)*

   Borrowing the maximum amount available to you may indicate that you are pushing the limits. If you borrow a little bit, and pay it off quickly, that shows you're in control of your debt.

   ➔ How much of your available credit (the amount allocated to you on your credit card) are you using?

3. **Length of credit history**

   *(less important—****15 percent*** *of your score)*

   The longer your credit history, the more information lenders have to make a decision.

   ➔ How long have you had credit accounts?

4. **New credit inquiries**

   *(less important—**10 percent** of your score)*

   Too many applications at once can raise concern that you don't have control of your spending.

   - How often do you apply for new credit cards or loans?

5. **Credit mix**

   *(less important—**10 percent** of your score)*

   This shows you can handle different types of borrowing.

   - Have you had different types of credit (car loan, credit cards, mortgage)?

Scammers can try to get loans or credit cards in your name if they have your personal information. If you don't need new credit soon, it's smart to put a "freeze" on your credit. To do this, contact the three credit bureaus (Equifax, Experian, and TransUnion) by phone or online.

A freeze means no one (not even you) can open new accounts while it's on. You can "unfreeze" with your password or code when you need a loan.

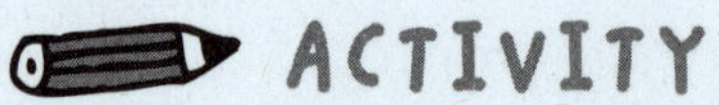

Why Does Your Credit Score Matter?

Having a good credit score makes adult life easier, but did you know it can also help make your dreams come true? Let's circle back to our earlier chat about what you want to do when you grow up, and figure out what kinds of loans you might need to make your dreams a reality!

1. Start by completing the following prompts:

   In 10 years, I'll be __________ years old.

   At that point, I plan to be (check all that apply):

   - ☐ Going to college or trade school
   - ☐ Enlisting in the military
   - ☐ Working part-time
   - ☐ Working full-time
   - ☐ Other

   ____

At that time, I would like to (check all that apply):

- ☐ Have a job (specify) ______
- ☐ Have a credit card
- ☐ Have a car (specify kind) ______
- ☐ Run my own business (specify) ______
- ☐ Other ______

In 15 years, I would like to (check all that apply):

- ☐ Work as a ______
- ☐ Be married/have a partner
- ☐ Have children
- ☐ Buy a home
- ☐ Have a cool vehicle (specify) ______
- ☐ Travel the world
- ☐ Other ______

2. Now, look over the goals and dreams you have. Let's say your goals are to go to trade school, start your own business, and buy a home. Think about what you might need to make these dreams happen. Now, brainstorm specific ideas for reaching your top three goals!

   Example

   Goal: *Go to Any State Technical Institute to become an electrician.*

   What financing you'll need: *Savings, loans, scholarships, and a part-time job to pay for tuition, books, meal plan, transportation*

   How you can get there: *Get good grades, work and save, research and apply for loans and scholarships, start building credit*

☆ Goal 1

____

What financing you'll need:

____

____

____

How you can get there:

____

____

____

☆ Goal 2

____

What financing you'll need:

____

____

____

How you can get there:

____

____

____

☆ Goal 3

____

What financing you'll need:

____

____

____

How you can get there:

____

____

____

CHAPTER 7

DEBT EXPLAINED

What You Need to Know

When used wisely, debt can be a helpful tool, like when you borrow money to build credit or buy a house. But borrowing too much money can cause problems and cost you a lot in interest—remember that Nintendo Switch we financed in chapter 4 (see page 56)?

Understanding Debt

Debt is money you borrow with the promise that you will pay it back later. Debt can be both good and bad. Let's explore how.

Good debt: This is debt that can help improve your future or help you earn more money. Some examples include:

- Student loans: Student or college loans can help you get an education to get a specialized, higher-paying job that you love in the future.
- Mortgage: Buying a home costs a lot, but it can be a great investment, because homes often increase in value over time, especially if you find a good deal or make smart improvements to the home.

Bad debt: This is debt that hurts you or messes things up in your future. This could mean borrowing for things that aren't necessary or that lose value quickly, not paying your debts, or borrowing at a high interest rate. This debt can be difficult to pay back. Some examples include:

- Credit card debt: This debt is risky, especially when you use it to buy things you don't need or can't afford to pay for. Credit cards typically charge a very high interest rate, so you can end up paying way more for the items than they actually cost.
- Payday loans: These are quick loans with high interest. These can seem helpful when you need quick access to cash, but they may be hard to pay off due to the high interest charges.

Debt Adds Up

As a kid, you probably don't have any debt yet. But, in a few years, you might get a credit card, buy a car, or have to pay for rent or tuition. When you have all these debts to pay back, a big chunk of the money you earn might go toward paying off those debts. This leaves less money to pay for fun stuff, lifestyle expenses, and investments.

Let's look at how debt adds up.

1. Think about your future goals, then fill in the blanks.

I just got a great job as a/an ____________________________. It pays $1,000 a week, or $4,500 a month, after taxes! I only pay $1,000 a month in rent, $300 on groceries, $225 to repay my college/trade school loan, $75 on my credit card bill, and $200 on other things like clothes and outings. With this new job, I plan to buy some fun things, too, including an awesome new ____, which will probably cost around $________________ a month.

2. Now, fill in the following chart:

Monthly Debt Payments	
Rent	$1,000
Groceries	$300
College/trade school loan	$225
Credit card bill	$75
Miscellaneous	$200
New item (fill in here):	$
Total Monthly Debt Payments	$

3. Now, subtract your total debt payments from your monthly income.

Income $ ______________

- Debt $ ______________

= $ ______________ Money left

As you can see, debt adds up, even when you get a nice paycheck!

Here's the moral of this activity: Debt is paying for your past when you could be investing in your future.

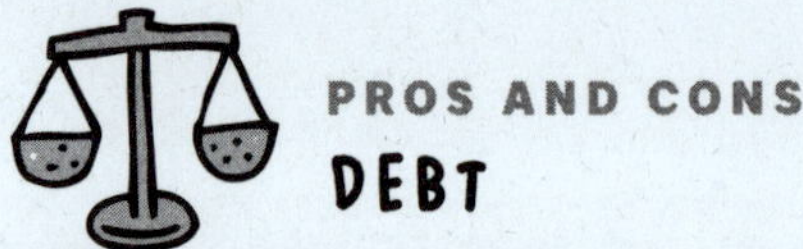

PROS AND CONS
DEBT

Much like good and bad debt, here are pros and cons to using debt as a tool:

PROS

- Debt can give you access to expensive things you might not be able to pay for with cash, like college, a home, or a loan to start a business.
- College debt can result in a future higher income and a fulfilling career.
- Having a mortgage for a house means you're not paying money to a landlord to rent a place to live. When your mortgage is paid off, you own your house. Homes often sell later for more than their purchase cost.
- A loan to start your business can give you the kick-start you need to get it off the ground. Many entrepreneurs have turned a small business loan into a multimillion-dollar enterprise!

CONS

- Debt can add up quickly, especially with interest or a missed payment.
- By taking on debt, part of your current income goes toward paying that debt, so that money can't be used for something you need now.
- The higher the interest rate on the debt, the more you'll pay over the item's original cost.
- For all these reasons, debt can make it hard to save money and get ahead.

ACTIVITY

See Loan Interest in Action

You have your heart set on a new $2,400 gaming computer. You've saved about $1,200, but it's going to take you another six months to save the rest. Your uncle said he'll put the purchase on his credit card, but you have to pay it off within a year. The credit card company is charging 15 percent interest.

How much would you have saved if you paid for the computer with cash?

___

What are the pros and cons of each decision?

___

___

___

Which choice would you make, and why?

___

___

PART THREE

INVESTING YOUR WAY TO WEALTH

CHAPTER 8

FIRST STEPS IN INVESTING

Making Your Money Work for You

It's time for the big score—investing! Investing helps your money grow over time, but in a bigger way than savings can. The sooner you start, the better. In this chapter, you'll learn about different ways to invest, how to handle the ups and downs of investing, and why investing now can set you up to be a millionaire in the future!

Understanding Investing

Investing is a way of putting your money to work for you. Over time, your money grows from your investments, kind of like a plant growing from a seed. Instead of you doing all the work to earn and save more money, your money starts doing some of the work for you.

If you earn $10 from babysitting and keep it in a safe, of course, it stays $10. But if you invest it, you're planting that $10 like a seed of opportunity that can grow over time without you having to add more to it.

Here are some fundamental concepts of investing:

- When you invest in something, you are buying a “piece” of whatever you invest in and hoping that its value will grow in the future. For example, when you buy Amazon stock, you own a piece of Amazon. If you own Amazon stock, when people buy stuff from Amazon and the company makes more money, you earn money, too.
- Risk. Investing comes with **risk**, meaning you take a chance that the value of your investments will grow, but it doesn’t always. So, when you plant a seed, but then there is a flood, your seed doesn’t grow like you had hoped. With investing, there is typically a lot of risk in the short term and less risk in the long term (more to come on that!).
- Return. Your **return** is the money you make from your investments. If you buy a share of stock for $5, and then next year it’s worth $7, that extra $2 is your return.

Time Is Your Superpower

The longer you leave your money invested, the more it can grow. The investment’s value might go up and down—sometimes drastically—but if you invest wisely and are patient and give it time, the investment’s value usually grows to more than what you started with.

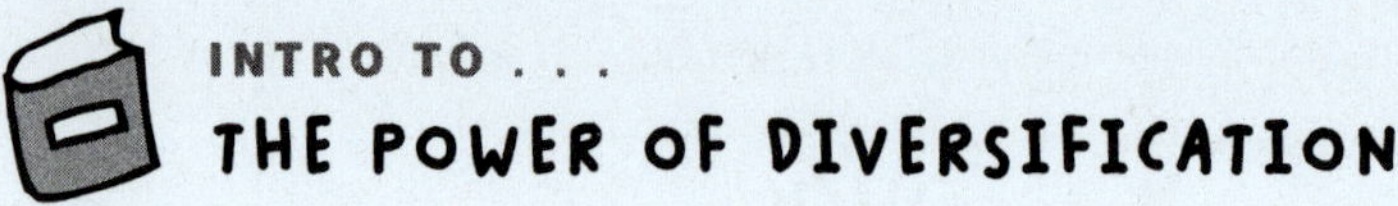

INTRO TO . . . THE POWER OF DIVERSIFICATION

Imagine you're loading snacks into your backpack for a sleepover. You love chocolate, so you only pack chocolate bars. When you get to the sleepover, you leave your backpack in the hot summer sun, melting all the bars. Well, now you have no snacks.

If you had packed chocolate and nuts, chips, pumpkin seeds, and crackers, you would still have the other snacks to enjoy even if the chocolate melted. That variety is **diversification**.

Investing is similar. Instead of putting all of your money into one company or stock, you spread it out across different ones. That way, if one company doesn't do well, you still have other investments that may perform better.

So, if you only own McDonald's stock, but fewer people buy Big Macs this year, the value of your stock could go down. But, if you also own Nintendo and Apple stocks, they might be doing great. When you diversify, or spread your wealth across different companies, all your money isn't being risked based on just one company doing well.

The Benefits of Investing Early

Want to know one of the smartest money moves you can make? Start investing early! In this section, I'll show you an example of how time and patience can help your money grow. In fact, you'll see how two people who invest the same amount of money end up with very different results.

Abhik starts investing during his freshman year in high school, when he starts working as a tutor. He invests 10 percent of his income every time he gets paid, which allows him to invest $50 per month for four years until he goes to college.

Abhik's facts:

- Starts investing at age 14
- Invests $50 per month for four years, for a total of $2,400
- Earns an annual investment return of 9 percent
- Stops investing after age 18, but keeps the money invested until age 30

Abhik's best friend, Tate, spends all of his money on V-Bucks and other fun things. Once he sees how Abhik's investment has grown, he starts investing the same $50 per month, but doesn't start until age 20.

Tate's facts:

- Starts investing at age 20
- Invests $50 per month for four years, for a total of $2,400
- Earns an annual investment return of 9 percent
- Stops investing after four years, but keeps the money invested until age 30

They both invested the same amount over four years, but Abhik started earlier. So who ends up with more money? Because he began six years sooner, Abhik's investments grew much more than Tate's.

At age 30, Abhik has over $3,000 more, even though both invested $2,400 over four years. Why? His money had more time to grow with interest—he started earlier and let it grow longer.

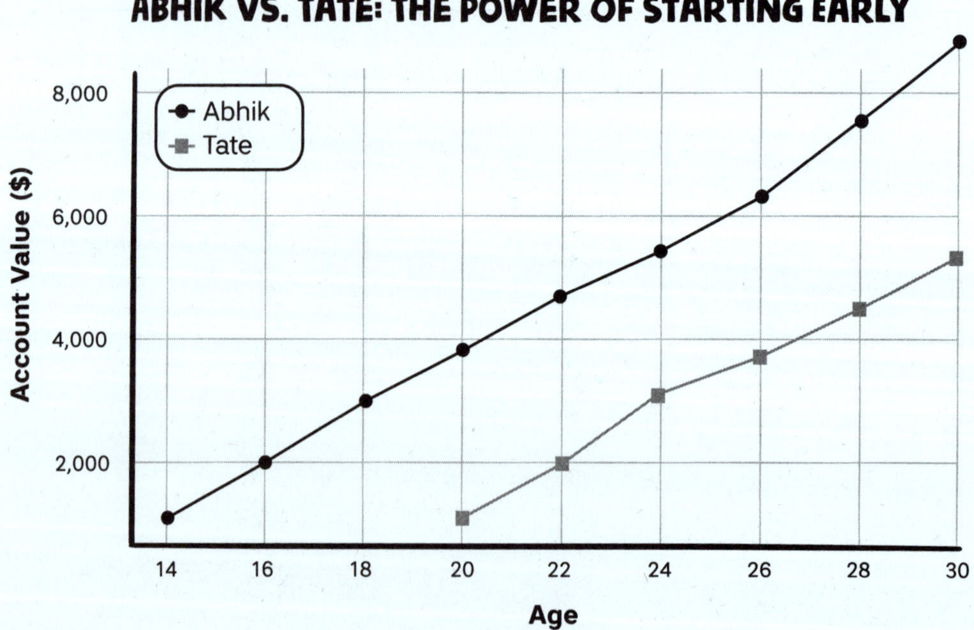

Brand Detective

Branding is everywhere! What is branding? Branding is how a company tries to make you remember them and want to buy their stuff. For example, you may recognize the Nike Swoosh logo and their "Just Do It" saying—this is branding.

With that in mind, your job is to find five to ten different brands or logos out in the world. Whether you're at school, driving somewhere, or just hanging out at home, keep an eye out for brands in different places. You might find them on someone's feet, on a cereal box, or on the side of the road. List the brands you find here. Then, using the internet, look up the companies you spotted and see how their stocks are doing. (You may not find all of them—privately owned companies don't sell stock.)

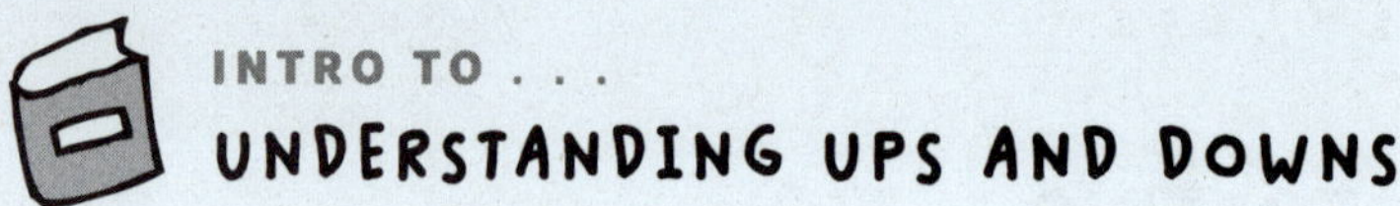

INTRO TO . . .

UNDERSTANDING UPS AND DOWNS

Investing comes with ups and downs—this is called **volatility**. Stock prices can change a lot, even in just a few hours.

Think of the stock market as a roller coaster. Sometimes it goes up (fun and exciting), sometimes it goes down (scary), but then it comes back up. The difference: The market can be bumpy day-to-day, but over 10 or more years it usually climbs. The key is to stay invested through the good and bad—you wouldn't jump off a roller coaster mid-ride!

BULL AND BEAR MARKETS

Over 10 years, the stock market usually has seven or eight great years (a **bull market**) and two or three bad ones (a **bear market**). But by the end, the market is higher than where it started.

It's like climbing a mountain: Some parts are steep, some flat or even downhill, some slippery—but overall, you're still going up.

The stock market is volatile, with prices rising and falling. But if you're patient and don't panic, you usually end up with more money in the long run.

Align Your Investments with Your Values

Earlier, we talked about values and that they are things that matter to you. They help you decide how you want to live your life. Here are a few examples of values:

- Honesty
- Kindness
- Generosity
- Responsibility
- Creativity
- Fairness
- Happiness
- Humor

For example, if you like to share and help others, you might value kindness, generosity, fairness, or all three.

When choosing the companies you invest in, it's important that their business goals and mission align with your values.

Consider this: If you care about healthy food but you invest in a junk food company, that doesn't align with your values. This can make you feel uneasy, because you're putting your money into something you don't believe in.

But, if one of your values is caring for animals, you might look for companies to invest in that supply quality animal goods. Likewise, if one of your values is helping people, you might want to invest in companies that support good causes, or companies that give to charity and treat their employees well.

So, what do *you* value? Here's a bigger list of common values. Circle the five values that describe you best, or add your own.

Authenticity
Achievement
Adventure
Authority
Autonomy
Balance
Beauty
Boldness
Compassion
Challenge
Community
Contribution
Creativity
Curiosity
Determination
Fairness
Faith

Fame
Friendships
Fun
Growth
Happiness
Honesty
Humor
Influence
Justice
Kindness
Knowledge
Leadership
Learning
Love
Loyalty
Openness
Optimism

Peace
Pleasure
Popularity
Recognition
Religion
Reputation
Respect
Responsibility
Security
Service
Spirituality
Stability
Status
Success
Trustworthiness
Wealth
Wisdom

Source: James Clear website: Jamesclear.com/core-values

Now, make a list of companies that you feel align with your values.

COMPANY NAME

VALUES WE SHARE

COMPANY NAME

VALUES WE SHARE

COMPANY NAME

VALUES WE SHARE

COMPANY NAME

VALUES WE SHARE

COMPANY NAME

VALUES WE SHARE

COMPANY NAME

VALUES WE SHARE

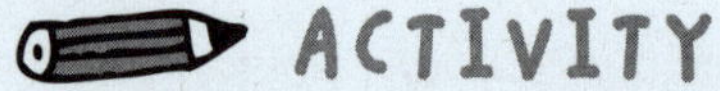

Start Investing Today

Are you excited about investing, but not sure where to start? You're in the right place—read on!

There are different types of investment accounts that can be used based on **when** you want to use the money in the future and **what** you want to spend it on.

For example, if you are saving money for your future retirement, you could invest the money inside a *retirement account*, such as an individual retirement account (IRA) or Roth IRA. Retirement accounts come with rules that you shouldn't take the money out of the investment until you are at least 59 1/2 years old, so you wouldn't want to put money there that you want to spend before that age.

A *brokerage account*, in comparison, is an investment account that doesn't have age restrictions. So, if you are investing money that you plan to use **before** retirement, you might invest funds in this type of account.

If you are saving for college or trade school, there are special accounts just for that goal called 529 Plans.

Now, we'll explore how to research, choose, and open an investment account (with the help of a trusted adult). Here are the steps to work through together:

1. **Think about your goals.** Decide why you're investing and what the money will be used for in the future. This helps determine what type of account to set up. For example:
   - If you plan to invest this money for retirement, a retirement account, like a Roth IRA, might be a good choice.
   - If you plan to invest this money to buy a car in five years, invest the funds in a brokerage account, not a retirement account.
   - If you plan to use these funds to pay for college or trade school, you might want to open a 529 education savings account.
   - If you plan to use this money to buy something later this year, you shouldn't invest the money at all; instead, keep it in a savings account.
2. **Decide where you will open your account.** Once you know what type of account you are opening, work with an adult to decide where to open it. Several companies offer kid-friendly investment options. These include Fidelity, Schwab, Greenlight App, Acorns Early, or Vanguard. Consider:
   - Minimums: Do you need a certain amount to get started?
   - Fees: What are the monthly fees, charges, or trading costs?
   - Security: Is the platform safe, insured, and well known?
   - Ownership: Who owns the account? When do you get control of it? (Many companies have **custodial** accounts, meaning the adult is the owner, or has custody of the account, and then it becomes yours at a certain age, such as 18 or 21.)

3. **Choose your investments.** When you put money into an investment account, you have to choose what investments you want in the account. You then use the cash you deposit to "buy" the investments. There are two ways to do this:
    - You can do some research and invest in individual company stocks, like Microsoft, Starbucks, or Wendy's.
    - You can buy a mix of investments by using an index fund, mutual fund, or exchange traded fund (ETF). Index funds, mutual funds, and ETFs are like buying a basket full of a lot of different stocks. For example, the S&P 500 index fund owns the 500 largest stocks in the United States. By investing in the S&P 500 index fund, you own a piece of all 500 of those companies. An investment company or financial planner can help you choose which is best for you.

CHAPTER 9

FROM STOCKS TO REAL ESTATE

Understanding Investment Opportunities

Investing has its own special language, but don't fear—I'm going to break it all down in this chapter. You'll learn helpful investing terms, explore different types of investments, and discover when using each type makes sense. You'll even get to choose your adventure, investment style!

Understanding Investment Opportunities

There are lots of different types of investments. Here are the most common investment types to know:

- **Stocks:** We've discussed that when you own a share of stock in a company, like Amazon, you own a piece of that company. When that company does well, your stock value goes up. When that company is doing poorly, the stock value may go down.
- **Bond:** Buying a bond is like giving a loan to a company or the government. When you buy a bond, you give that company or government money, which they promise to pay back with interest over a certain period of time.

- **Mutual fund:** A mutual fund is like a basket of a bunch of different stocks, bonds, or a mix of both that is managed by a professional money manager. The manager chooses which stocks and bonds to include in the fund, and you own those when you buy the fund.
- **Index fund:** An index fund is very similar to a mutual fund, but instead of a money manager choosing the stocks, it tracks a certain **market index**. There are different market indexes that track certain stocks. For example, the S&P 500 index fund tracks the 500 largest stocks in America. When you own the S&P 500 index fund, you own a piece of all of those companies, and the value goes up and down as they do.
- **Exchange traded fund (ETF):** This is also a basket of stocks or bonds like a mutual fund or index fund, but ETFs trade like a stock. The value of stock changes every minute of the day when the stock market is open. For example, if you buy a share of Apple at 10 a.m., the price might be different than if you bought it at 12:45 p.m. When you buy a mutual fund or index fund, they only have one price per day, which is determined at the end of the trading day. When you buy an ETF, the price updates all day long.

Why choose one type over another?

- **Individual stock or bond:** With a stock, you're investing in just one company. With an individual bond, you are holding a loan for one company.

  √ ***Why choose it?***

  Because you really believe in the company and want to take a chance it will do well for a bigger reward.

  × ***Why not?***

  If something bad happens to that company, your money could shrink fast. For example, if you buy Nintendo and then Nintendo gets in trouble for something, the stock price (and your money) might go down rapidly. In the case of a bond, the company might not be able to pay back the "loan." However, government bonds are insured, so your investment is protected.

- **Mutual fund/index fund/ETF:** With a mutual fund, index fund, or ETF, you get a taste of a lot of different companies, and it's more diversified.

  √ ***Why choose it?***

  When one company does badly, you still own investments in a lot of other companies in the fund, which could do well and keep your money growing, so it's less risky.

  × ***Why not?***

  You don't get to choose your investments—someone else does it for you. If you only want to invest in companies you believe in, you may prefer individual stocks. It can also be hard to see exactly which companies you own inside the fund.

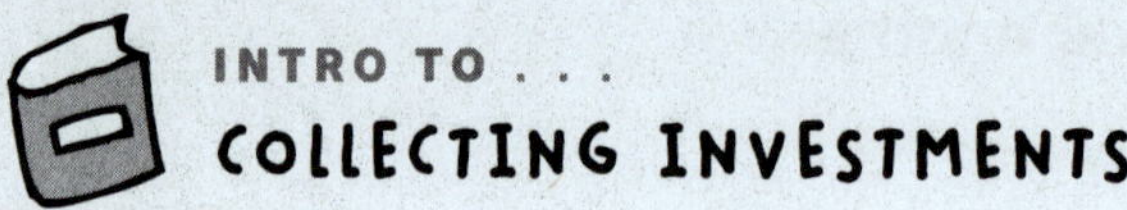

COLLECTING INVESTMENTS

There are other types of investments called **physical assets**. These are items you own that you think might be worth more money in the future. Here are some examples of physical assets:

- Art: paintings, sculptures
- Cars: old, rare, or classic cars not being made anymore
- Collectibles: silver coins, baseball cards, Barbies, Beanie Babies
- Jewelry: diamonds, gold, silver, rings, necklaces, vintage pieces
- Rare items: stamps, vintage toys, wine, comic books
- Real estate: land, property, buildings, houses

Why would someone want to invest in physical assets?

- They want to be able to see it. They feel more comfortable with an investment they can see, touch, or hold.
- They enjoy them. If you love art, you can invest in it and display it.
- These items might keep growing in value. Some things are not made anymore, like certain cars. If you have one, it might keep growing in value because there aren't many available.

Why wouldn't someone invest in physical assets?

- They can be hard to sell. To make money on these investments, you have to find someone who wants to buy them from you, at their increased worth.
- You have to take care of them, and keep them safe and clean. In the case of cars and real estate, you might need to make repairs.
- You could lose them. You could misplace items, or they could get stolen or lost in a fire.

Not All That Glitters Is Gold

Most items we own are not considered investments, even though they cost money and have value. Rather, they are things we buy to use, enjoy, or wear; not things we buy hoping they'll grow in value later.

Sure, some items can be sold to someone else when you're done using them, but usually you'll get less money for the items than you originally paid for then.

Some things that are not investments:

- The bike you ride to school
- The video games you play
- Your favorite hoodie
- Your toys and stuffed animals

Building Your Investment Portfolio

What is a **portfolio**? Easy! Your investment portfolio is a collection of all the things in which you are invested. Think of it like a backpack for your money.

Just like your backpack holds all of your different school supplies, your portfolio holds all of your different investment accounts (Roth IRA, brokerage account, for example) and investment holdings (stocks, bonds, index funds, for example).

Now that you know about the different types of investments, which are you interested in adding to *your* portfolio?

1. Check off all that apply:

- ☐ Stocks
- ☐ Bonds
- ☐ Index funds
- ☐ Mutual funds
- ☐ ETFs
- ☐ Art
- ☐ Other
- ☐ Jewelry
- ☐ Collectibles
- ☐ Real estate
- ☐ Land
- ☐ Cars

____

2. Write down which of the investment(s) from the previous page you'd like to own in your portfolio.

______________________'S PORTFOLIO

You may start with one investment, but keep going. Within a few years, your portfolio might have several types of accounts and several types of investments as it grows and you add to it over time. They're all steps in the right direction—to financial freedom!

Tech-Based Investments

The world of money is always changing, and there are some new kinds of investments that didn't exist when your parents were kids. These include forms of digital money, online art, and even pretend land in video games. Tech-based investments are one type of fintech, which is technology used to manage finances. These are all examples of **fintech**, which is short for financial technology and is used to describe all the ways technology is used to keep track of and use money. New forms of investing can be exciting and cool, but they are also risky and unpredictable. Let's take a look at some of these new and interesting ways people are investing today, and some of the terminology that goes along with it.

- **Cryptocurrency (crypto):** This is a digital form of money that is not made by the government. You can't hold it in your hand; instead, it's used and traded online. It's kind of like video game coins, but for real money.
- **Blockchain:** This is a type of digital "notebook" that keeps track, in a safe way, of who owns what cryptocurrencies. Every time someone makes a trade or buys some digital currency, the information is recorded in this "notebook." Instead of one person holding the notebook, everyone gets a copy. Once something is written in the notebook, it can't be erased or changed. It's called "blockchain" because it's made of blocks of information linked together like a chain!

- **Sustainable/impact investing:** These type of investments are in companies that try to help the planet or people, like using clean energy that doesn't harm Earth. This could be a good investment strategy when you want your money to grow while also doing good in the world.
- **Non-fungible tokens (NFTs):** These are digital collectibles, like owning a special Pokémon card, but only online. NFTs can be art, funny pictures of pets, or even music that only lives in the digital world. People can buy, sell, and create NFTs and can make money if others want to buy them.
- **Virtual real estate:** This is pretend land in online worlds (like in a video game). It's not real, like the land your home is on, but people can still buy and sell it online.
- **Crowdfunding:** This is an investment in which lots of people chip in small amounts of money to help a person with their venture (such as making a movie) or help a company get started. Sometimes, you get to be a part of that company in the future. If the company or enterprise does well, it could be a good investment. If it doesn't, you could lose all the money you put in.

Be cautious with "new" investments. Some people have made money with these investments, but a lot of people lose money. It's important to understand what you are investing in, ask a lot of questions, and talk to a trusted adult before putting money into something new.

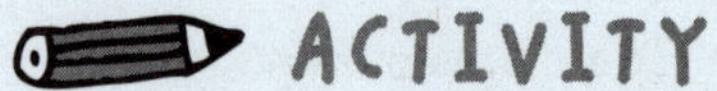

Fact-Checking Investments

Before putting money into any investment, it's important to do some fact-checking. You want to make sure the investment is safe, smart, and right for you. Just because your friend invested in it doesn't mean it will be a good investment for you. Which investment are you interested in? Let's do a fact-check.

1. **Choose the investment you'd like to investigate** (*examples: mutual fund, Microsoft stock, index fund or ETF*).

   ____

2. **Find the facts (who, what, where, how).**

   Who is this kind of investment right for? Consider the length of investing time and the amount of risk desired.

   ____

   If this is a company, what does this company do or make?

   ____

   Where can I buy it?

   ____

   How do I buy it?

   ____

3. **Do a risk assessment** (circle Yes or No).

Is this investment within my budget?	Yes No
Could I lose money?	Yes No
Does the value change often?	Yes No
Does this investment have a track record of growing over time?	Yes No
Does it sound too good to be true? (If yes, it probably is!)	Yes No
Does it promise to make me rich fast? (If yes, this could be a scam!)	Yes No
Do I understand this investment well enough to explain it to others?	Yes No

4. **Check your references.**

- ➜ Talk with a trusted adult about your idea.
- ➜ Research the investment online.
- ➜ Check Investor.gov to make sure it's not a scam.

Investing on the Go: Apps to Kick-Start Your Investing Journey

In today's world, you can easily open accounts and track them through apps on your phone or tablet. Here are some examples of investment apps for kids and some features of each. Be sure to get permission and supervision from your parent or a trusted caregiver.

Acorns Early (Acorns.com)

- **Best for:** Investing for kids—buying an investment and holding on to it for a long time
- **Features:** Kid debit card with money management features; parents can invest in custodial brokerage accounts for the child
- **Ages:** Any
- **Cost:** Family Plan costs $5 per month

BusyKid (Busykid.com)

- **Best for:** Earning money through chores and investing it
- **Features:** Chore app with a spending card
- **Ages:** 5 through 17
- **Cost:** Annual fee around $50 per year

Fidelity Youth Account (Fidelity.com/go/youth-account/overview)

- **Best for:** Teens wanting to start investment accounts
- **Features:** Teen-owned account with parent supervision; learn to save and invest money
- **Ages:** 13 through 17
- **Cost:** No fees, except any internal fees within the investment holdings

Greenlight (Greenlight.com)

- **Best for:** All-in-one money management or allowance management (spending, saving, and investing)
- **Features:** Kids can invest in real stocks and ETFs with parent approval; comes with a debit card
- **Ages:** 6+
- **Cost:** $4.99 per-month subscription, with optional add-ons

Stockpile (Stockpile.com)

- **Best for:** Giving stocks to kids as gifts to learn through real investing
- **Features:** Kids and parents learn and invest together—need only $1 to start
- **Ages:** Any
- **Cost:** No monthly fee, but $0.99 per-trade fee

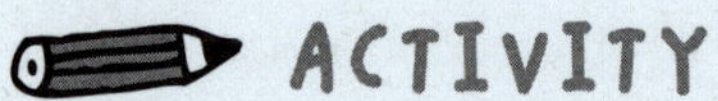

Testing Investing—Choose Your Adventure!

You earned $500 from your summer job, and now you're on a quest to invest it and make it grow! What will you choose to invest in?

Your favorite stock? Real estate? A new business? You get to decide, and see how it goes!

The Starting Line

What do you want to do with your $500?

a. Choose a company stock to invest in.
b. Invest in an index fund.
c. Put it into a savings account.
d. Buy supplies to start a dog-walking business.

If you chose A: You invested in a company stock.

The company stock could go up or down at any time, so let's **flip a coin** to see what happens after one year of owning the stock:

- ✓ **Heads:** The company released a new product that was a huge success. The stock is up, and your shares are now valued at $750!
- ✕ **Tails:** The company released a new product that was a flop. The stock is down, and your shares are now valued at $420.

What will you choose?

- ➜ Continue to own the stock, and let it grow or recover—
  Go to **Ending #1.**

OR

- ➜ Sell the stock, and invest in something else—
  Go back and choose Option A or B.

If you chose B: You invested in an index fund.

The stock market did well this year, so the $500 you invested in the S&P 500 index fund is now worth $560.

What will you choose?

- ➜ Remain invested, and let the fund keep growing—
  Go to **Ending #2.**

OR

- ➜ Sell the index fund, and use the money for something else—
  Go back and choose Option A, C, or D.

If you chose C: You put the money into a savings account.

You decided to keep the $500 in your savings account and earn a little bit of interest. After one year, you now have $502.

What will you choose?

- ➔ Keep it in savings to use to buy a new PlayStation and games—Go to **Ending #3.**

  OR

- ➔ Continue holding the money in your savings account—Go to **Ending #4.**

  OR

- ➔ Invest it to try to earn more money—**Go back to Option A or B.**

If you chose D: You bought supplies to start a dog-walking business.

You used your money to purchase nice dog leashes, poop bags, doggy treats, and a portable water bowl, and spent the rest on advertising.

You end up with three customers, who each pay you $50 per week to take their dogs on regular walks. In one year, you have made $2,600 in your business.

What will you choose?

- ➔ Keep $500 in savings for your emergency fund, and invest the rest in an index fund—Go to **Ending #5.**

  OR

- ➔ Use the profit to start another business—Go to **Ending #6.**

Endings

Ending #1—Investing Whiz

You know the stock price will go up and down, but you don't panic. You did a lot of research on the company you invested in and believe the company will continue to grow in value. Your patience pays off! At the end of three years, the stock that you bought with $500 is now worth $800!

Ending #2—Long-Term Investor

You're investing for the long term. You chose an index fund that is a diversified mix of companies in the United States. After three years, the $500 you invested in the index fund is now worth $680!

Ending #3—Saving for Something Big

When you're saving for something big that you want to buy soon, it's best to keep those funds in a savings account instead of investing them. You are a smart saver, so the money was there when you were ready to make the purchase.

Ending #4—Cautious Saver

You've chosen to keep your money in savings, earning some interest. At the end of three years, your $500 has grown to $510. Remember that having a cash cushion is a good thing, but investments are where your money can really grow over time. Maybe consider investing just a percentage of your savings until you feel more comfortable with investments.

Ending #5—Savvy Business Owner

You invested in your business, and it has paid off! You now have a steady stream of income that has far exceeded your initial investment. You keep some money in savings for business supplies and emergencies, then put the rest of your profit to work by investing it! The $2,100 you invested from your profit has grown to $2,700 in three years. After such a good investing experience, you plan to invest more of your future profits!

Ending #6—Business Enterprise

You are a savvy business owner and are creating jobs and income for yourself and others. The businesses have good years and bad years but are profitable overall. You get to create your own schedule and work on your terms. Your streams of business income allow you to invest more and more money over time. Well done!

CONCLUSION

You made it to the end of this book! Give yourself a big high five, because you've learned more than some adults know about how to earn, save, and invest money like a future millionaire.

In part one, you learned to build a solid financial foundation. Sadly, money doesn't grow on trees, but you learned how it can grow when you make smart choices. We discussed different ways to earn money, either by working for someone else or starting your own business, and how to keep your money safe. We even talked about taxes and building a résumé to show off your skills and achievements.

Then, in part two, you mapped out your millionaire path. You created a budget, learned how to sort out needs from wants, and found out which spending style you have. You learned how to be a savvy saver by understanding how to handle debt and grow your credit score. Without this basic knowledge in place, becoming a millionaire is almost impossible, but you now know what you need to do to pave your path to financial success.

Finally, in part three, you became an investor, even if just on paper, and you've certainly got the training. You learned investment lingo, explored different ways to grow your money, and got to choose your adventure to see how your choices can shape your future.

As you can see from all the options, there is no one "right" way to grow your money. It just takes smart decisions, patience, and practice. Being money savvy doesn't mean you don't make mistakes. It means you are curious, make thoughtful choices, and learn as you go. You've already taken the first steps. Now, keep going, keep growing, and use your money to build the life you want.

Congratulations for finishing this book and taking the first step toward becoming a millionaire. Now, go put your knowledge to work for you and your promising future!

RESOURCES

Bankaroo.com

A virtual bank for kids that helps them learn about money management by tracking allowances, savings goals, and spending in a fun, interactive way.

Bizkids.com

An educational website that teaches kids and teens about money, business, and entrepreneurship through videos, lesson plans, and games.

ChooseFI.com

A financial independence podcast and community offering tools, strategies, and stories to help families optimize spending, save more, and reach financial freedom.

Consumerfinance.gov/consumer-tools/money-as-you-grow

A resource from the Consumer Financial Protection Bureau (CFPB) offering age-appropriate activities and guidance to help parents and caregivers teach kids money skills from early childhood through young adulthood.

Easypeasyfinance.com

A kid-friendly site that breaks down financial concepts into simple, short videos, blog posts, and quizzes for children, teens, and beginners.

Instagram.com/moneybossmom

Jamie Bosse's Instagram account featuring family finance tips, money lessons for kids, and real-life insights from a financial planner and author.

Miltonthemoneysavvypup.com

A playful and educational site centered on Milton the Money Savvy Pup, offering children's books, activity books, and free resources to help kids learn smart money habits.

PBSkids.org

An interactive and educational platform by PBS featuring games, videos, and activities that teach children a wide range of topics including basic money skills.

Sheeksfreaks.com/about-dan-sheeks

Learn about Dan Sheeks, a high school teacher and advocate for teen financial independence, and his work empowering young people to build wealth early in life.

Thefourmoneybears.com

A children's book and financial literacy movement that introduces kids to the four basic functions of money—spending, saving, investing, and giving—through storytelling.

Thesimplestartup.com/about

A program and workbook designed by Rob Phelan to help teens start their first businesses and learn entrepreneurship through simple, actionable steps.

Apps

Acorns Early (Acorns.com)

Kid debit card with money management features; parents can invest in custodial brokerage accounts for the child; monthly fee applies

BusyKid (Busykid.com)

Chore app with a spending card and savings tracker; annual fee applies

Fidelity Youth Account (Fidelity.com/go/youth-account/overview)

Teen-owned account with parent supervision; learn to save and invest money; no fee to start

Greenlight (Greenlight.com)

Kids can invest in real stocks and ETFs with parent approval; includes a savings tracker and comes with a debit card; monthly fee applies

MyFirstNestEgg (Myfirstnestegg.com)

Savings tracker and financial literacy resources for kids and parents

Stockpile (Stockpile.com)

App for gifting stocks to kids to learn through real investing; no monthly fee but a small per-trade fee applies

Websites

BreadBox.money

Saving and investment resources and articles for kids

RetailMeNot (Retailmenot.com)

Coupon codes that can be copied for online and in-person shopping

Trustpilot (Trustpilot.com)

Offers company reviews to help you learn about companies to make wise shopping decisions

Credit Reporting Agencies (Check Your Credit Score and Freeze Your Accounts)

Equifax (Equifax.com)

Experian (Experian.com)

TransUnion (Transunion.com)

Books for Kids

Ages 9–12

Danny Dollar Millionaire Extraordinaire: The Lemonade Escapade by Ty Allan Jackson

The Golden Quest: Your Journey to a Rich Life by David Delisle

Grandpa's Fortune Fables: Fun Stories to Teach Kids About Money by Will Rainey

Make Your Own Money by Ty Allan Jackson

Money Skills for Kids by Ferne Bowe

The Startup Squad: Party Problems by Brian Weisfeld and Nicole C. Kear

Ages 13–17

Essential Money Skills for Teens by Jordan Wize

First to a Million: A Teenager's Guide to Achieving Early Financial Independence by Dan Sheeks

From Piggy Banks to Stocks: The Ultimate Guide for a Young Investor by Maya Corbic

How to Money: Your Ultimate Visual Guide to the Basics of Finance by Jean Chatzky, Kathryn Tuggle, and the Hermoney Team

Malik's First Job: Financial Principles for Teens by Kerwyn S. Phillip

Millionaires for the Month by Stacy McAnulty

Money Skills for Teens by Aspire-Axis

INDEX

ACKNOWLEDGMENTS

I would like to thank the amazing Zeitgeist team at Penguin Random House for taking a chance on me and helping bring this book to life! Thank you for your patience as I learned your systems and processes—and for your encouragement every step of the way. A special thank-you to Angelica Martinez and Sarah Curley for your thoughtful guidance and belief in this project from the very beginning.

To my kids, Ellie, Auggie, Oscar, and Landry—thank you for being my favorite test subjects and giving honest (and often hilarious) feedback as I shaped the content of this book. I love being able to teach you and other children the importance of being money savvy from a young age.

To my husband, Weylan—thank you for being endlessly supportive, especially when I take on extra projects during our already jam-packed schedules. I couldn't do this without your encouragement and partnership.

To my coworkers and clients—thank you for believing in my mission and sharing my books with your families and friends. Your support means everything.

To the mentors, teachers, and librarians who sparked my love for learning and financial literacy—thank you for planting the seeds that led to this book.

And to YOU—thank you for reading this book and taking steps to build a brighter financial future. Whether you're a young reader, a parent, or an educator, your commitment to financial education is powerful. You're not just learning—you're changing the trajectory of your life, your family, and generations to come.

It's my hope that this book sparks curiosity, confidence, and conversations that last a lifetime.

ABOUT THE AUTHOR

JAMIE BOSSE, CFP®, RFC, CCFC, is an author and mom of four kids! She loves teaching people how to be smart with their money so they can reach their goals—like buying a house, saving for fun adventures, or investing for their future.

She practices financial planning at CGN Advisors, where she works with individuals and families to help them better understand, manage, and improve their financial situation.

Jamie has a passion for mentoring and financial literacy and is the author of *Money Boss Mom*: *Helping Young Parents Be the "Boss" of Their Financial Future*, as well as the Milton the Money Savvy Pup children's book series.

Hi, parents and caregivers,

We hope your child enjoyed *Investing for Tweens*. If you have any questions or concerns about this book, or have received a damaged copy, please contact customerservice@penguinrandomhouse.com. We're here and happy to help.

Also, please consider writing a review on your favorite retailer's website to let others know what you and your child thought of the book!

Sincerely,
The Zeitgeist Team